TUNES
FOR BEARS
TO DANCE TO

TUNES
FOR BEARS
TO DANCE TO

RONALD WALLACE

UNIVERSITY OF
PITTSBURGH PRESS

Published by the University of Pittsburgh Press, Pittsburgh, Pa. 15260
Copyright © 1983, Ronald Wallace
All rights reserved
Feffer and Simons, Inc., London
Manufactured in the United States of America

Library of Congress Cataloging in Publication Data

Wallace, Ronald.
    Tunes for bears to dance to.

    (Pitt poetry series)
    I. Title. II. Series.
PS3573.A4314T8   1983   811'.54   82-23893
ISBN 0-8229-3481-7
ISBN 0-8229-5353-6 (pbk.)

The author would like to thank the following publications for permission to reprint some of the poems appearing in this collection: *The Atlantic, The Chariton Review, Cincinnati Poetry Review, Midwest Poetry Review, The Midwest Quarterly, New Letters, The Paris Review, Poem, Poetry Northwest, Quarry West, Sou'wester,* and *Tar River Poetry.*

The following poems originally appeared in *The Chowder Review:* "Birds of Paradise," "Lies," "Myrrh," and "Sestina for the House." "Picture of Molly, Age 4" is reprinted from *The Little Magazine.* "The Belly Dancer in the Nursing Home" and "Arranging the Pig" first appeared in *The Madison Review.* "A Collection of Rocks" was first published in *The Poetry Miscellany.* "Clean" and "Novelties" originally appeared in *Other Islands.* "The Facts of Life," "Fat: In Love," and "Up in Minnesota" are reprinted from *Poet Lore.* "The Dentist's Disappearance" and "Picture of Two Bugs, Hugging" first appeared in *Prairie Schooner,* copyright © 1982 University of Nebraska Press. "April" and "Wild Strawberries" are reprinted with permission from *Quarterly West. Southwest Review* first published "The Assistant Professor's Nightmare." "And on Earth" was originally published in *Wisconsin Academy Review,* December 1981, Vol. 28, No. 1. "Falling" is reprinted with permission from the September 1980 issue of *Yankee Magazine,* published by Yankee Publishing Incorporated, Dublin, N. H. 03444, Copyright 1980.

The author would also like to thank the Wisconsin Arts Board (in conjunction with the National Endowment for the Arts), the Graduate School Research Committee of the University of Wisconsin, and the Wisconsin Foundation, for their generous support.

*The publication of this book is supported by grants
from the National Endowment for the Arts
in Washington, D.C., a Federal agency,
and the Pennsylvania Council on the Arts.*

for my family

Human language is like a cracked kettle on which we beat out tunes for bears to dance to, when all the time we are longing to move the stars to pity.

—Gustave Flaubert

CONTENTS

CONTENTS

I

The Origin of the Instruments

THE ORIGIN OF THE INSTRUMENTS

1.

Expectant, breathless,
the long slide extended,
the mouthpiece first meeting the lips,
then the first gulp of air, the first cry,
the first tuneless red moment,
trombone.

2.

The plucked voice complaining,
whining, striking the small scale of rage.
This, too, even, lovely, this harping.

3.

The mouth open on the belly,
blowing, an abrupt and amateur blat,
the texture of wet flesh and giggle:
the sax.

4.

The grass full of blackbirds.
Placed between thumb and thumb,
green reed, brash grackle,
clarinet.

5.

The bent thumb tucked under
the blunt middle finger,
now thumping the taut cheek,
thin membrane, tympanum,
the mouth with its small, toned O.

3

6.

The maple seed under the tongue,
thin zither, dizzy tickler,
hissing its breathy, arresting
whistle of fizz and spittle.

7.

The mouth a small bottle,
corked with a short finger
popping the melody out.
Or say a viola, the cheek
plucked like an untuned string.

8.

The first hurt, brassy scrape,
the tight fist to the lips,
the stiff valves of pain,
the stung mouthpiece, the howl,
the trumpet.

9.

Fingernails on the table,
their small moons and sorrows,
thin sticks, traps,
tapping and dancing,
these brushes, these drummers,
these snares.

10.

Darkness. Quiet.
Mouth, hand, and breath.
This silence. This unfinished
symphony. This pause. This rest.

AT THE ST. LOUIS INSTITUTE OF MUSIC

When Mr. Croxford
flicked his skinny wrist,
and the metronome began
its slow tick in his throat,
I knew that I was lost.
My thick hands tripped and stumbled
over the deviant keys,
my sour stomach off-key,
out of tune.
Outside, the day grew taut,
the fall air thin as wire,
and his voice, that cracked
and raspy sounding board,
sent me home.

All week I'd hear him clicking
out in center field, as
bases loaded, I'd pop up.
Or in the lunchroom,
flirting with the girls,
I'd feel his thin wrist
measuring my tongue until
his cracked voice rasped me back
and there I'd be again, legs
dangling from the stool,
wishing I had practiced.

Until one day they caught him
in the washroom
in a stall with Porky Brown,
and my short unhappy practice sessions ended.
I can't say I wasn't glad, or that
I felt much pity for him:

I made first string and several girls
and easily forgot him.
Yet, years later, safely married,
on days flat and diminished,
as I practice my profession
in the silence of my room,
I miss the crazy bastard,
and wish him back to abuse me
into song.

GRANDMOTHER GRACE

I didn't give her a good-bye kiss
as I went off in the bus for the last time,
away from her house in Williamsburg, Iowa,
away from her empty house with Jesus
on all of the walls, with clawfoot tub and sink,
with the angular rooms that trapped all my summers.

I remember going there every summer—
every day beginning with that lavender kiss,
that face sprayed and powdered at the upstairs sink,
then mornings of fragile teacups and old times,
afternoons of spit-moistened hankies and Jesus,
keeping me clean in Williamsburg, Iowa.

Cast off, abandoned, in Williamsburg, Iowa,
I sat in that angular house with summer
dragging me onward, hearing how Jesus
loved Judas despite his last kiss,
how he turned his other cheek time after time,
how God wouldn't let the good person sink.

Months later, at Christmas, my heart would sink
when that flowery letter from Williamsburg, Iowa
arrived, insistent, always on time,
stiff and perfumed as summer.
She always sealed it with a kiss,
a taped-over dime, and the words of Jesus.

I could have done without the words of Jesus;
the dime was there to make the message sink
in, I thought; and the violet kiss,
quavering and frail, all the way from Williamsburg, Iowa,
sealed some agreement we had for the next summer
as certain and relentless as time.

I didn't know this would be the last time.
If I had, I might even have prayed to Jesus
to let me see her once again next summer.
But how could I know she would sink,
her feet fat boats of cancer, in Williamsburg, Iowa,
alone, forsaken, without my last kiss?

I was ten, Jesus, and the idea of a kiss
at that time made my young stomach sink.
Let it be summer. Let it be Williamsburg, Iowa.

IN THE DRESS FACTORY

We unrolled the bolts of material.
Harry worked faster than the rest,
fascinated with the language of color:
Cranberry, he said. *Cranberry.* And
Mahogany, Chartreuse, Cerulean.

Louie Prince, his nose blown out
by acne, would talk about his wife
and their hot nights. He knew
the virtues of Westinghouse fans,
the intricacies of condoms,
the sensuousness of sweat
in the close St. Louis summers.

And there was Al, who could not
cut a straight line, who liked
to drop his pants for the women,
"adjusting his jock," and fondling
the bolts of material.

Meanwhile, the women,
hunched up like scraps of cloth,
sat in the corners tying knots
and sewing, their lips buttoned shut,
their quick eyes sewn in place,
only their fingers flitting
in the still dark.

So I spent the summer with them,
unrolling those long, hot days
on the table, learning from the men
how to cut things off,
learning from the women
how to sew things up, how to
tie things all together.

A COLLECTION OF ROCKS

Every day, the summer I was ten,
I packed two lunches and rode my bike
across campus to my father's office.
On the way I stopped at the Geology Building
to collect discarded rocks:
limestone, basalt, fool's gold, granite,
junked in a clutter of jagged rubble,
labeled with their angular, mysterious names.
Then late, out of breath,
my hands covered with dust,
I arrived at the Law Building
where my father sat
in his wheelchair, in his office,
propped up, rigid, waiting for me,
a thin smile splitting his face.
The few words between us
were heavy and monotone, gray.
We never much opened up
to each other. I wonder if he knew
why I came. And then after lunch
I was back at the dump,
cracking open the geodes,
filling my empty lunchbags up
with the dullest of treasures, singing
amethyst, rose quartz, carnelian, lapis,
the summer my father was sick and dying,
the summer I learned those names.

WORRIED

This was in 1958. We were worried
about taking showers for the first time
with the other guys, and whether
we'd be laughed at; worried
about the old bus driver
who smoked large cigars
and kicked us in the pants
and out the door sometimes before
the bus had even stopped; worried
about the sad and queasy mysteries
of puberty.

Meanwhile, down in the subbasement,
the workmen, finishing off the shelter,
were drunk on our stocked beer;
far off in Russia the Commies
were smiling past their arms;
and down in Pruitt-Igoe
the quiet Negroes were rising, fighting
their own cold war.

Nervous in the suburbs, we worried
about Eisenhower, Elvis, the moon, rock and roll,
black slacks, penny loafers, and how to make
our short hair stand on end
as we named and named our enemies:
Khrushchev, Mel Oppenheim the Principal,
our fathers, authority and fear.

Until one day in '58 I remember
telling Nancy Farr I'd fuck her, long
before I knew or could. And then
she told my father. I remember
him wobbling, drunk on his cold
anger, his black stare, remember
him falling toward me, crutches flailing
in slow motion, two hundred pounds of dead
weight, slowly falling toward me
as I deftly stepped aside,
and didn't break
his fall.

UP IN MINNESOTA

Three men from the next cabin
haul my father up on their backs
like a slab of venison,
walk him toward the lake,
deposit him. Like some
strange fish or
a crab back in water,
he crawls deeper, water
spouting from his mouth.
Finally he can stand,
his legs growing from the sand
like seaweed. It is worth
it, he thinks, as his wheelchair,
cane, and crutches, disappear
in the deep water, and the future,
clutching its bedpans, catheters,
needles and pills goes under.
Giddy and buoyant on his
wasted legs, he balances,
remembering how it was
before everything got him down.
He grins. Calls for me to follow him.
My mother gives me a push, and
somehow, I swim.
When I finally clamber
up on his shoulders,
I know we are going to drown.

FATHER AND SON

He sat at the foot of my bed
with authority, I thought, not love,
counting me down to sleep,
his stiff crutches propped in the doorway,
their shadow flat on my back, until
there was nothing I could do
but let go and float out of myself
toward that unattainable
galaxy of pretense—love, and sleep.
But when he was finally satisfied
that I'd gone off, sometimes he'd weep.
I never knew why. And so, years later,
as I sat by his high bed,
watching him drift off beyond me,
I let him go, as he let me,
my silence flat at his feet.
I didn't try to call him back
from that calm, untroubled sleep.

TUNES FOR BEARS TO DANCE TO

For the third time in ten years
my father is dying. First
bladder infections, then pneumonia, and now
a single improbable bedsore, and once more
the doctors are shaking their stethoscopes
and muttering "no hope."
My mother says, as she's said before,
she'd rather he were gone
than lying helpless forever
with his catheter and pills
and the fixed routine his only
dependable visitors.
But I don't know.
Has his paralysis spread so far
he can't move even us?
Ten years ago I wept, and careless
of embarrassment or futility,
railed at the pale, indifferent sky.
Five years ago I grieved
more for myself, for my cool, detached
poetic eye.
Today, I am merely reasonable and calm
as the inevitable 2 A.M. telephone
tells me the terrible news:
a festering bedsore has burst
to the surface, shredding his skin
like lettuce; his tailbone is
a thin spike of rot.
The doctors are appalled.
It should never have happened,
should have been
avoidable. They are wrong.

It is never avoidable.
The human heart one day stops beating
out its tunes for bears to dance to,
as if it knows that only silence
could finally move the stars to pity.

TICS

When my father first fell under his weight,
when everything got him down
and he took it out on me,
knocking my elbows off the table,
slamming my hands at the piano keys,
cuffing my butch-waxed hair,

my eyes began to flex and squint,
my mouth and nose elongate in
a rhythmic mockery of a yawn,
my small teeth grate through sleep,
my morning face an assortment of contortions
that twitched me through the year,

until one night I watched him twitch
through a mockery of sleep,
his lungs a ruckus of mucous,
his loud face knocked with pain
until everything habitual ceased
in that terrible silence of peace.

This morning the tics come back to me.
How love inflects the memory,
mouth and eye.

BIRDS OF PARADISE

for W. E. W., 1924–1981

In this artificial
sea-green and aqua chapel
with its satin and velvet air,
its birds of paradise and mums,
my father lies in his mahogany coffin
like some wax manikin or pear.

They've touched up his birthmark and blemishes,
they've parted his hair
on the wrong side,
uncrimped his illegible hands,
given him a stranger's suit to wear,
his kingdom finally come.

Numb, insufficient, I drop my mother's arm,
turn my back on death's accessories.
I want to slap the understanding faces,
tear the imperishable voices,
rend the familiar prayer,
our father . . . our father. . . .

Until, for one sweet moment I see him
driving his motorized wheelchair
out of that sea-green room,
beyond their careful arrangements,
grinning, out of tune. . . .
And then he's gone.

NUMISMATICS

When my father dies, and we pry open
his small locked box, we find:
a double eagle, three silver dollars,
some liberty standing halves and quarters,
a few uncirculated Mercury dimes
shining in the costly afternoon light.
And in a yellowed envelope,
sealed with brittle tape and grime,
eighty-nine paper milk bottle tops,
marked Pevely Dairy, St. Louis, one pint.
Thus, as the sun sets, worn in the orchard,
and we stare at the valuable coins,
watching their light fade flat as cardboard,
the eighty-nine milk-stained wafers shine.

MYRRH

In the Sunday School Christmas Pageant
I was always the third king,
draped in my bedsheets,
my fake beard protruding
stiff as an accusation—
Why did you make me do it?—
my hands sweating and cold,
my small heart spinning,
while somehow from out of my mouth
the thin tune shimmering,
Myrrh is mine . . .
as I dreamed of the time
I'd be too old for all this,
too old to listen to you.

Last night I dreamed
I called you long distance,
something I hadn't done in years.
It had been so difficult
getting you to the phone, someone
holding it up to your ear,
and usually a bad connection.
This time they gave me a stranger,
a mistake, a misunderstanding, I reasoned,
but when I repeated
your name in the phone,
when I shouted your name at the silence,
I knew I would wake up, taking
my part in this heartless season,
draped in my sweating bedsheets, and
the clamor of bitter perfume.

AFTER MONET

The day is humid, a threat
of rain: beer, leather, feed, and sulfur
loll in the languorous air.
Inside, in the museum,
people stretch and shuffle in line,
an undulation of yawn and muffle
among the Rodins and Moores.

Jostled by elbows, stomachs, and smells,
I wait, dull, impatient, until my mind's eye
blinks far enough back that
the line is a mass of color, of pigment,
each person a brush stroke, a slash
in the shimmering air, my eye
the only frame keeping them whole.

Now they could be the blue haze on the Seine,
a row of golden poplars,
a gray footbridge at Giverny,
a pathway of fire through irises.
I think of Monet, how he was called "just an eye,"
how Renoir said "all art is inimitable,"
how Monet said "it drives you mad."

Now the line blurs and quickens.
People float past the sequence
of morning on the Seine, rippling
their small appreciations, or gather
in front of haystacks, shocked, fingers aflutter,
or, stiff as poplars, leaf
through brochures, blond hair and skin shimmering,

until they are lilies in this blue room,
are floating-heart and spatterdock
bobbing on the water of my eye,
until odor and sound and texture and color
are light in the luminous air, and I leave them there
in that flowering room, in my painting of Monet's painting,
keeping my own weathers and seasons, my own atmospheres,

and walk back outside where the sky,
for all my imagination, is painting itself gray
with chemicals, evening, and rain, where
there is nothing to do but stroke my way home
through the huge, unavoidable dusk,
through the aging, cataracted sky,
through this muddy, unmanageable palette.

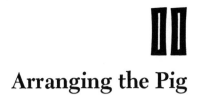

Arranging the Pig

THE ASSISTANT PROFESSOR'S NIGHTMARE

I'm giving the Faulkner lecture as usual,
all the pencils nodding their heads
in astonishment: Wallace is brilliant,
Wallace is wise. My sure voice filling
their notebooks up when
back row, aisle three, Kevin McGann,
graduate teaching assistant, begins
to shake his ominous head. A white balloon
drifts out of his mouth, and oozes
to the front of the room: ridiculous,
it says, ridiculous. Suddenly confidence
slips out of my voice, sits down
in the front row, snoring.
My stomach and the room give out,
my small words stumbling on. Soon
all of the pencils are wagging their fingers,
shouting with their black tongues.
Two hundred points rise up at me
as I grow smaller and smaller, my thin
voice humming like a gnat. I look
for a safe way out of this, but
lost in grammatical confusion,
my sentence goes on and on
and I disappear in a flurry of notes,
my fury and my sound crossed out,
the room closed up like a book.

CONVERSATION WITH THE MAKER OF CLICHÉS

Up here above the treetops:
green heads, you say, *green hair.*
Why not green water waving?
A thousand locusts hovering? Green air?

The branches, now, the bark. You say:
the long arms of dark women, mossy skin.
Why not the hard scars of barnacles?
Dead husks? Stuck wings molting?

Now the roots and trunk. You say:
the long body, crossed thighs, soft toes.
Why not a sunken Spanish galleon?
Dead cicada dreaming toward the sun?

But now the leaves like fingers
open in the poem, combing their
green hair, green arms holding my throat.
They love me; won't let go.

IN A PIG'S EYE

I am a male chauvinist pig,
they say. Suddenly, I am
snuffling and grunting, my long tongue wallowing.
"Week-week! Week!" I say.
See? I don't take them seriously,
they say. No men take them
seriously. Suddenly I am
sober as stone. Deep wrinkles chiseled
in my brow. I could not crack
a joke if I wanted to and I don't.
See? I am impassive. I don't listen,
they say. Suddenly I sprout ears,
ears on my head, down my neck,
back, arms, and legs, until I am
all ears. See? I'm not serious,
they say. I am two-faced. Suddenly
while my one face nods its stone head
my other face snorts off toward the kitchen,
its snout full of aprons and babies.
See? I don't take them seriously,
they say. I keep sticking myself in
where I'm not wanted. I'm a real prick,
they say. Suddenly I am
blushing, filling with blood, until
I decide it's time to stand up for myself.
See? I'm about to spout off again.
I'm so predictable, they say.

ARRANGING THE PIG

Start with mud. Then add swill.
Wallow in it. Soon it will
take shape in your brain. Now stuff
in some coarse bristles and tufts.
Add tusks if a boar, teats if a sow,
stiff as funnels. Now
breathe in through the snout, not out,
singing, "Week-week! Week!" Root
for yourself. Now imagine a sty,
some ripe fruity pigshit to lie
in, a farmer to scoot you down.
Let him call you Pig, Hog, or Swine.
When your mate lifts you off your feet
by any other name you'll smell as sweet.

A HOT PROPERTY

I am not. I am
an also-ran,
a bridesmaid, a finalist,
a second-best bed. I am
the one they could just
as easily have given it to
but didn't.
I'm a near miss, a close second,
an understudy, a runner-up.
I'm the one who was just
edged, shaded, bested, nosed out.
I made the final cut,
the short list,
the long deliberation.
I'm good, very good,
but I'm not good enough.
I'm an alternate, a backup,
a very close decision,
a red ribbon, a handshake,
a glowing commendation.
You don't know me.
I've a dozen names,
all honorably mentioned.
I could be anybody.

NOVELTIES

for Dave

The doorbell grins.
When you tweak its chin
the whole room opens,
a box full of laughs.
He waves you on in,
his hand stuck out like a socket.
When you shake it
little z's snag in the air,
your palm full of bees.

Now he shuffles you around the room
like a deck of defective cards,
his eyes bright as flash paper.
When he gives you his metal and velvet rabbits,
his ceramic chipmunks and squirrels,
when he sticks a cold water tap
on his forehead, and says
it's a drain on his brain,
when he says with his X-ray specs
he sees through you,
you know it's time to complain.

So he changes his tactics,
his fast talk sticking
its elbows in your ribs,
spilling its invisible ink on your shirt.
He gives you his
foaming sugar, stink loads,
instant worms, exploding pen;
his sneeze powder, black soap,
vampire blood, and dribble glass;
his snapping gum, itching dust,
talking teeth, and snake nut can;

until even the chair cushions
blat with embarrassment,
the plastic flowers squirt,
and you feel clumsy, incompetent,
like a sore thumb, rubber, engorged,
the room a huge lucite ice cube,
and you the proverbial fly.

But just when you're thinking
the stain of such jokes
will take days to wear off,
his laughter a mote in your eye,
he hands you the forgotten toy
of your childhood, wound up,
ready to go, and you know
that your life's a dark closet
you've been locked up in
as punishment for growing old.
When you strike that first match
that sputters into snakes
and hand him his own large cigar,
it's you who, tickled
after all these years,
finally light up and explode.

"YOU CAN'T WRITE A POEM
ABOUT McDONALD'S"

Noon. Hunger the only thing
singing in my belly.
I walk through the blossoming cherry trees
on the library mall,
past the young couples coupling,
by the crazy fanatic
screaming doom and salvation
at a sensation-hungry crowd,
to the Lake Street McDonald's.
It is crowded, the lines long and sluggish.
I wait in the greasy air.
All around me people are eating—
the sizzle of conversation,
the salty odor of sweat,
the warm flesh pressing out of
hip huggers and halter tops.
When I finally reach the cash register,
the counter girl is crisp as a pickle,
her fingers thin as french fries,
her face brown as a bun.
Suddenly I understand cannibalism.
As I reach for her,
she breaks into pieces
wrapped neat and packaged for take-out.
I'm thinking, how amazing it is
to live in this country, how easy
it is to be filled.
We leave together, her warm aroma
close at my side.

I walk back through the cherry trees
blossoming up into pies,
the young couples frying in
the hot, oily sun,
the crowd eating up the fanatic,
singing, my ear, eye, and tongue
fat with the wonder
of this hungry world.

FAT: IN LOVE

My legs grow thick as an elephant's.
My jowls wrinkle and lengthen.
Even my voice, gone blunt as a trumpet,
sags, and loses shape.
Squat on the fat bed, eating,
my breasts bloated and swollen,
my heavy stomach hunkering,
I loll, baggy as old pants,
sweat dropping from me in globules.
And yet, when you arrive,
my smiling, thin Houdini,
filling me with your sweet breath
and flesh, my ponderous body rises,
floats, and like a delicate aroma
vanishes in the thin stunned air.

HELP

This morning my socks
opened their mouths
and swallowed my feet;
the toothy zipper of my pants
closed upon my waist;
my T-shirt wrapped around me
like a tongue.

Outside, everyone,
already half-eaten, clung
to jaws of cars,
to streets' moist lips,
to buildings burping their fill.

From inside my clothes
I called for help until
you found me, love,
and we pried open
all those mouths until
you held me safe and naked
in the warm fork of your arm.

THE DENTIST'S DISAPPEARANCE

for E. N. Vogel, 1932–1980

Outside my office they mock me,
I'm a quick one-liner, a joke,
an oral mechanic or tooth doctor,
my diplomas worth no more than smoke.
And yet when they come to me, furtive,
their loud mouths hanging open,
begging, impatient with pain,
they expect me to be a magician,
mint-breathed, gentle as rain.
When I give them what money buys,
my bright drill whistling like a wizard,
my own pain locked in their eyes,
what do they know of my heart,
its beatings, its dark cavities?

Now I'm through with their lipless language,
their throaty, innocuous talk.
I've filled my last tooth, and locked up
my receptionist, hygienist, and clock.
Let them sit in my office
stiff with compressed air and Muzak,
their futures grown gray with decay.
I'm away where no one will know me,
where my hair and nails will grow dangerously
long, my scrubbed hands turn to clay.
Let my absence shine like an incisor
inside them. Let them, in silence, pray
for me, plucked out in my wisdom,
my life gone rank, and gay!

BIRD STUDY

One of the penalties of an ecological education is that
one lives alone in a world of wounds.—Aldo Leopold

Called by the common
robin, jay, as well as the more
spectacular oriole and towhee,
Clark flits from tree to tree
through fields of bird's-foot
violet and puccoon,
through oak and pine woods,
swamp and marshland,
gawky with binoculars, all
elbows and awkwardness,
eyes cocked at the sky,
ears tuned to the cry
of the pileated woodpecker,
the black-billed cuckoo.

He's got 58 kinds by breakfast—
opening his notebook on a litany
of birds, intoning the sparrows:
vesper, lark, chipping,
clay-colored, swamp, song.
My own notes like jays
clattering across the page,
cowbirds robbing his words,
I search my bird book, thinking:
Loons, crazy as; Ducks, odd.
Until he falls
silent as a mid-morning forest,
his tongue limping like a killdeer
when anyone threatens conversation.

I think as a child he must have been
"bird-brained," "for the birds,"
hawknosed and friendless, wrens
nesting in the crofts of his arms,

37

inept and furtive, fluttering
on the edge of anybody's attention.
And now as he sits muttering
gutturally into his plate,
stiff as a bittern, arms tucked in
close to his notebook, what
does he know of the blunter connections:
the ruffed grouse drumming for his mate,
the tree swallows, high on a wire,
their flutter and thrum of copulation?

But there's something in silence.
Something in the simple
chickadee's two mournful notes,
the mourning dove's low quiet sigh,
that rivals the yellow throat's
baroque celebrations, that raises
my dull morning eye, until
I see Clark flying high beyond me,
beyond all showy display,
beyond any call or cry,
there with the wounded
great blue heron,
his slow wings echoing
over the hills from sky to sky!

BIRD WATCHER

for Mr. Carpenter, 1893–1975

Enthused by flickers and coots,
he rises at five
and bicycles out to the point,
his eyes full of birds.

His thin legs pumping like wings,
his voice a white note on the air,
I watch him from
my window overhead, disappear.

Later, after breakfast,
I hear him return,
his bicycle rattling like a cough,
his red face feathered with sweat.

He flits past my window,
breathless, absurd,
his arms waving wildly,
every finger a bird.

AND ON EARTH

The church is dark, heavy with weather and breath.
We sit wedged in the pews,
swaddled in winter coats, scarves, and gloves,
hugging our hymnals, our children
growing restless between us.

Outside, an ice storm
has shut down the city
and cut the electricity off.
Inside, the stars aren't working,
the whole nave nothing but dark,
until a custodian, drunk in the sacristy,
lifts his thin flashlight up.
In that uncertain beam
of intoxicated light
the pageant begins:

Up in the chancel
one angel bungles her lines
while another trips over her robes, ascending
the paint-stained ladder
to announce the coming of the Lord.
The three shepherds, lodged in the dark
at the back of the sanctuary, do not
hear them or start their long walk.
One pops his bubble gum, while another
adjusts his dish towel headdress
and the third fiddles with his crotch.

Meanwhile, Mary and Joseph are stuck somewhere
in the back seat of a snowbound Buick,
and the three kings, their gifts wrapped in tinfoil,
are at home in their kitchen,
in front of the gas stove, shivering.

Tomorrow, Christ will be born.
But tonight, unredeemed and awkward,
we squat on the hard pews
wondering why we've come
out in such weather
to watch the poor shepherds
watch their invisible flocks.

THE BELLY DANCER
IN THE NURSING HOME

The crazy ladies are singing again,
clapping their hands and gums to the music,
dancing their wheelchairs to and fro
with a frail and bony toe.
In the front row, some old men,
flushed with the heat of the season,
are thumping their tuneless canes and stumps,
driving old age and infirmity
out of the room like an unwanted guest.
Meanwhile, the belly dancer,
all sweat and sequins, muscles and skin,
ripples and pumps,
her skimpy metallic costume slipping
beneath her secret hair,
until even my father, slumped in his chair,
lifts his voice and quickens:
Goddamn! he sings. Look there!
Until we're all dancing and singing,
hips, breasts, and heads ringing
the immodest, unlikely air,
until the performance is over.
The women stiffen into their chairs;
the men lean back on their silence;
and my father folds up as in prayer,
with just enough breath left to whisper.
And sing. And dance. And swear.

CLEAN

Cleanliness is the yardstick of civilization.—Freud

At night, patient, serene,
dependable as weariness,
they slide their carts
stacked with the emblems of their profession—
their rags and brushes, bottles and sprays,
soaps and powders, sponges and plungers—
down the noiseless, darkened corridors
of your life,
empty of regrets or promises.
Although you never see them
scrub or polish, tidy or remove,
each morning your world,
left in fragments and loose ends
the day before,
is back in shape,
predictable, ordered,
clean as a new start.
You go on with your life
as if nothing had happened,
undiscriminating, dumb,
without thanks or reservations.

But some dark night
when the world has wound down
to an occasional tick of crickets
or the slow drone of a semi shifting down,
some insomniac night, lying in bed
with the clutter and baggage
you've dragged along with you
unwilling between the sheets,

you may feel a slight breeze
wipe silently over you
as you're quietly plunged into sleep,
and you may sense a thin spray of stars
waiting patiently
for the moon, that white sponge,
to wash through
you and your unclean incomparable dreams.

III

The Art of Love

LEARNING TO TALK

Your voice
is the first clean thing.
I want to fill it
with the syllables I've lost:
(those bright birds)
oriole, goldfinch, flicker,
swallow, linnet.

The afternoon wears off.
Time takes us by the hand
through the dark.
Your cries demand
firefly, twinkle, spark.

I open my old mouth:
your bright words flutter out.

PICTURE OF MOLLY, AGE 4

Picture this: a child with eyes as blue
as the first blue scylla of spring,
hair the color of oak leaves in the fall,
a voice as pure as bloodroot, and as clear.
A small bud of surprises;
a wildflower of light;
a poem you wish you had written,
and will take all the credit for.
In short: a child so beautiful
she could only be your own,
telling a friend outside your study door,
You can't read his books because
there are too many words
and there aren't any pictures at all.

ART WORK

My daughter is drawing a picture
of me, comical figure: my hair
a spike of asparagus, my face
a round tomato, fat and red,
my eyes two curvy worms
tugging at their hole, my mouth.
She is bending over this garden,
tending it carefully, absorbed
in her own small making.
I smile, and return to my larger work
where, later, I find myself
scratching my thick green hair,
squeezing my ripe plump cheeks,
my old eyes squirming away from me,
tugging at my blind mouth.

1001 NIGHTS

Each night I read you stories—
Sinbad, Aladdin, Periebanou, Periezade—
in that strange exotic language
you cannot possibly understand:
countenance, repast, bequeathed, nuptial,
what can these words be telling you?
What can they signify?
That I love you? That it's time to sleep?
Keep safe throughout this night?
And yet you will not let me simplify,
get angry if I explain,
and hang on every word as if
our lives depended on it.
Perhaps they do.
One day the stories will fail us,
there will be nothing left to tell,
another hand will rub your back,
another genii will rise.
But for now, sleep tight, sleep tight,
and dream of the singing tree,
the speaking bird, the golden water,
the stone that was your father
restored by morning light.

THE FACTS OF LIFE

She wonders how people get babies.
Suddenly vague and distracted,
we talk about "making love."
She's six and unsatisfied, finds
our limp answers unpersuasive.
Embarrassed, we stiffen, and try again,
this time exposing the stark naked words:
penis, vagina, sperm, womb, and egg.
She thinks we're pulling her leg.
We decide that it's time
to get passionate and insist.
But she's angry, disgusted.
Why do we always make fun of her?
Why do we lie?
We sigh, try cabbages, storks.
She smiles. That's more like it.
We talk on into the night, trying
magic seeds, good fairies, god. . . .

PICTURE OF TWO BUGS, HUGGING

Ladybugs, leafhoppers, salamanders, toads,
leopard frogs, dung beetles, spittlebugs, caterpillars,
whatever crawls, flies, hops, or skitters,
whatever is small, peculiar, unloved,
whatever makes your older sister scream and flee,
holds you quiet for hours.
Crawling through the tall grass,
buzzing along a pond or stream,
you find them and bring them lovingly home.

Emily. How close we came to giving you up.
At six months, white, unlovely as a slug,
the doctors clucking their tongues: *Microcephalic*.
The word, a brittle insect, crawled into our ears
as we pictured your skull gone
smooth as a shell, the sutures sealed too soon.
And then the months of waiting. Beetle-
browed, your face pinched and ugly, you were
shrill as a cicada. How I wanted
to swat you away, smash those cries
against wall or ceiling, take you by your
furry legs, and pin you, sprawling, down.
Meanwhile, in our mind's eye, you grew
queer as a thrips or mantis, your head
small as an aphid or gnat.
And we made our painful plans.

But now, at four, you are normal, lovely
as a butterfly, fluttering about the yard
after grasshoppers, dragonflies, June bugs: your
emerald, sapphire, gold. So easy to love you
now, no more skulking in corners, our dark
thoughts closing around us, our hearts working
their small mouths. And did you love us
then, as we love you now?
I remember the picture you drew
the day we knew you were healthy,
the picture of me and you. You said,
a picture of two bugs, hugging.

LIES

You bring it in out of our garden,
this warty clod, small pulsing lump,
so delicate and grotesque you could
squash it in finger and thumb.

You want him to stay. You say
you found him, he's yours.
I talk about rights of possession,
human and natural laws.

You don't listen:
Plopped in a makeshift terrarium
he sits, his sadness, you insist,
just my imagination.

Well. I'll learn to catch flies.
With my slow tongue
and his quick one
we'll dispel the princely lies.

Until he digs himself under the pumice
and dies.
Then I'll tell you of transformations,
of wonderful disguise.

LAPAROSCOPY

First, we make a simple incision in the navel,
less than half an inch.
Then, we fill the abdomen up
with carbon dioxide until
the body is light as breath,
the belly large and spongy as a sigh.
Then, we insert a thin pin of light
into the abdominal cavity,
the organs set aside now,
out of touch, the fallopian tubes
luminous, pellucid.
Then we peer through the navel,
thin window of imperfection,
and slip the children out
invisible as air. We pass
an electric current through their breathing,
tie off their thin insistence.

There may be complications:
a swelling below the collarbone;
a small lump in the throat;
a sad and puffy abdomen grown tender.
There is no need for worry.
They will pass with the CO_2.
Though later you may expect
a small lisp of tissue
to quicken in your belly, monthly,
as your small thoughts fill with children
and your body fills with eggs.

And maybe some dark night
somewhere inside sleep
you may see that thin incision
sewn shut, like the tiny sewn-shut mouths
of embryos, turn luminous, turn blue,
smile at you.

APRIL

Cedar waxwings
thrum in the viburnam,
their hooked beaks poking
a single berry back and forth:
the last remnant of autumn.
The air is a taut string,
plucked, ringing.

My wife says they are
kissing, making love,
her small words leaning
toward me. But I am
not so sure. I lean back
brusque, insistent.
They are only hungry.

Still, we watch together,
taut, her bent arm
hooked through mine, while
the thin air quivers
between us, and
my dull heart thrums
its stiff, invisible wings.

WILD STRAWBERRIES

In this weedy field somewhere inside marriage,
snuggled under thistles and nettles, we find them,
bright promises. Down on our knees like penitents
or children, we pick, our tongues puckered and bloodied,
our careless hands stung red, the sun plumping
ripe and peppery in the July sky.

This morning we fought over nothing
I can remember, pride springing up all around us,
with its barbs and hooks. Now all afternoon
I've been thinking how we'll grow old together,
our perennial violence and tenderness,
bearing less and less.

Back in the city, the markets stock strawberries
bred for safe shipment, long storage,
crisp and predictable in their stacked flats.
Here, as we carry our berries back to the cabin,
back to our dangerous lives,
we know they are so fragile and ripe

their own weight in the bowl could ruin or bruise them
beyond texture, or beauty, or definition.

SEPTEMBER RAIN

Last color bleeds from the trees,
the slow drip of rain, collapsing.
The feverish maples decline.
We pause to pick mushrooms,
stick into our sacks these
squat, warty, beige and tan hammers,
these spongy plungers and rams,
these alien, faceless denizens of damp.

They are not in our book.
As we walk through this flaccid rain,
this vague sense of loss and wrong,
we don't talk. But we wonder
about maples and mushrooms, about us:
Anything you can't name is dangerous.

FALLING

Move slowly up to the window,
breathe deeply and
slide through the glass.
You will feel the wind on your face
like a last kiss, the leaves
lisping encouragement beneath you.
Study the flight of dust,
the slow patience of clouds,
the determination of rain.
Take these for your answers.
Now step off the ledge. Think
how your life flies upward beyond you;
how silence unfolds like a knife;
how peaceful the dark earth, its turning.
Now open your hands.

SESTINA FOR THE HOUSE

October. They decide it is time to move.
The family has grown too large, the house
too small. The father smokes his pipe.
He says, I know that you all love
this house. He turns to his child
who is crying. She doesn't want to leave.

Outside in the large bright yard the leaves
are turning. They know it is time to move
down onto the ground where the child
will rake them together and make a house
for her dolls to play in. They love
the child. A small bird starts to pipe

his song to the leaves while the pipe
in the father's hand sputters. The father leaves
no doubt that he's made up his mind. He loves
his family; that's why they must move.
The child says, this is a wonderful house.
But nobody listens. She's only a child.

The father continues to talk. The child
cries, staring out at the Indian pipes
in her backyard, wondering if the birds of this house
will pack up their children, their nests, and leave
the old yard. Do birds ever move?
Do they know her sadness, her love?

Her father is smoking and talking of love.
Does he know what it's like being a child?
He knows she doesn't want to move.
She hates him sitting there smoking his pipe.
When has he ever been forced to leave
something he loved? He can't love this house.

The father sits by himself in the house
thinking how painful it is to love
a daughter, a house. He's watched her leave
saying she hates him. She's just a child
but it hurts nonetheless. Smoking his pipe
he wonders if he is wrong about the move.

Outside the bird pipes: Don't move. Don't move.
The bright leaves fall on the wonderful house.
And the child sits crying, learning about love.

THE ART OF LOVE

We get handwritten cards from the children:
Dear Parents, come visit our school—
our names painfully etched in crabbed script, the art
teacher's latest project. We say we would love
to come. We'll see Home Room, Art, and Music.
We promise to be there on time.

We've been talking a good deal these days about time.
About how when we were children
time was a kind of slow music,
a sure pulse of expectation, a school
in which, leisurely, we learned about love,
in which singing all day took no art.

The memory itself, we know, is all art.
It was never so happy as that at the time,
we remind ourselves, laughing, and love
wasn't easy, not even for children.
We remember those queasy afternoons after school:
the dark corridors of failure, of facing the music.

The first room we visit this time is Music.
An old upright piano, locked; art
work carved on the marred wooden school
desks; a metronome keeping the time
as we go through the motions of singing, the children
teaching us all of the songs that they love.

Valentines plaster the walls of the Art Room: Love
with its gaudy construction and fluff. No music
in these rough cuts and doilies the children
manufacture in the interests of "art."
It's getting late now, the time
moving faster, faster than it ever did in school.

But Home Room's the best thing in school,
they insist! We follow them out of love
through a motley of workbooks, torn papers, and time
tests, until memory turns up its old music
and everything blurs—Home Room, Music, and Art—
to the slow bobbing heads of the children.

And we know we would school ourselves in such music,
would cut out and paste up such love for all time,
would make a new start. Were we children. Had we the art.